Look at Me!

Jeff Newell
Illustrated by Barbara Hranilovich

Lisa drew a blue mouse.

3

The mouse ran off the paper.
"Oh, no!" said Lisa.

"Look at me!" said the mouse.

Lisa drew a yellow cat.
The cat ran off the paper.

7

8

"Oh, no!" said Lisa.
"Look at me!" said the cat.

Lisa drew a black dog.
The dog ran off the paper.

11

"Look at me!" said the dog.

"Stop! Stop!" said Lisa.
"Look at all the mess!"

Lisa drew a red aeroplane.
The aeroplane flew off the paper.

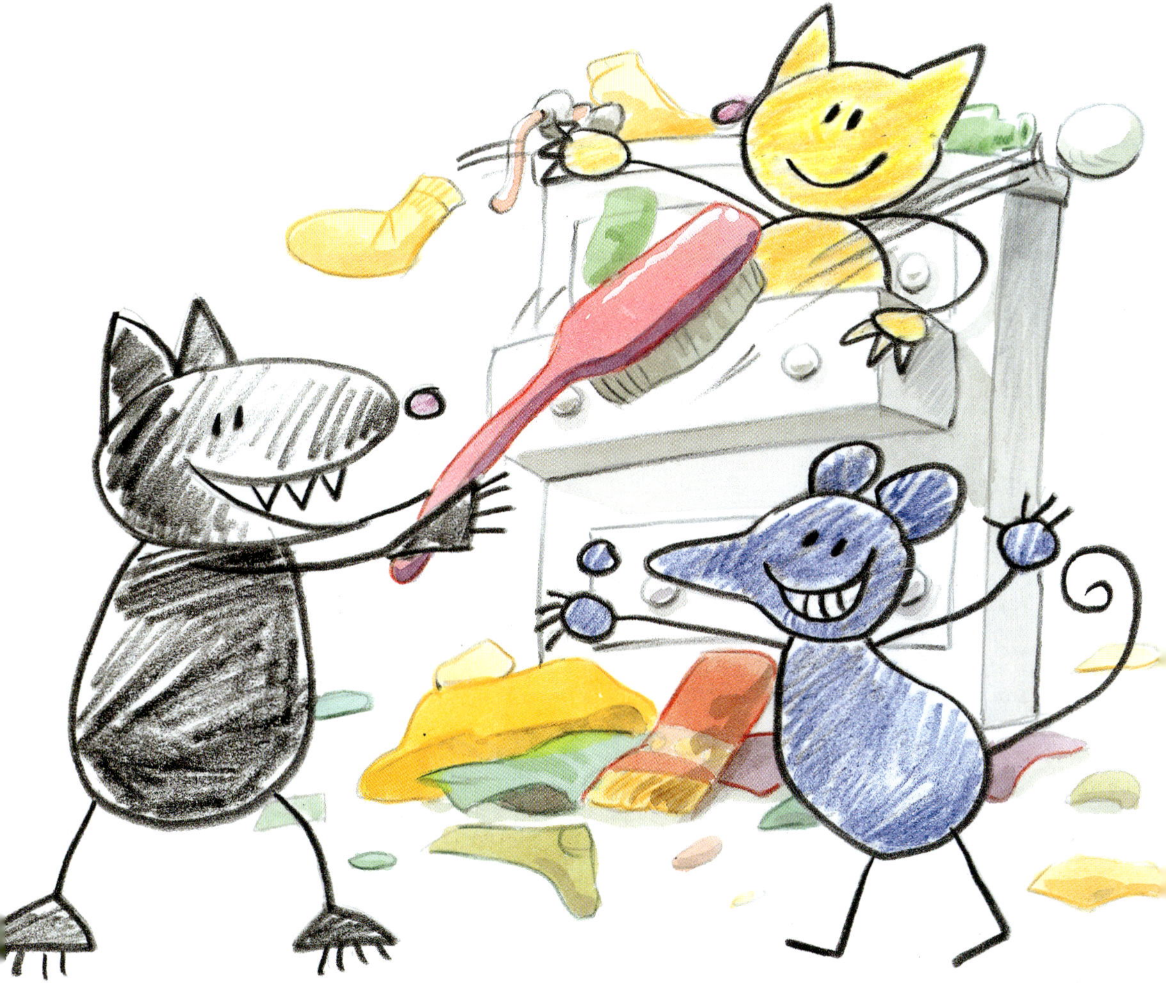

"Thank you!" said the dog and the cat and the mouse.
And they flew away.